Mother and Daughter

This painting of the relationship of a mother and daughter was commissioned as a double portrait in 1981.

The mother, with a reflected portrait of herself in the mirror, is in control of the scene. She is arranging flowers on a table built into the wall. The daughter is given freedom in the scene. She is there and not there.

The cool blue atmosphere of the wall paper enriches the scene.

The cover of this book is the daughter alone in a dominant, warm red atmosphere. The other colors relate to the red. The illusion of broken colors tries to catch the viewer's attention. The colors which come from light create the light.

Stare at the scene to obtain its full effects.

Aged and Ageless

Mother, mirrored on the wall,
Standing stately, standing tall,
You oversee this pleasant scene
And blend so well with blue and green.

Daughter, carefree — without care —
Your eyes are focused straight and nowhere.
How great is youth and youthful ways,
You glide and grow in a stack of days.

Each of you, although not aware,
Has captured the artist with your stare.
He has given you life besides your own,
An enduring age, though time has flown.

Womanhood now and from times untold,
You are more precious than precious gold.

Stepping Onto the Stage of Life

The young lady of this painting is Vincent's grandniece and the grand-daughter of his brother-in-law Fred Bakkes, our genius photographer.

The scene is a significant one. The house, like the young lady at the work of growing up, is under construction. Except for the floor and some planks, everything is in a vertical position. It matches the young lady's upright posture. How very much she is herself. From her head to her hands and to her sneaker-fitted feet, she oozes femininity and dignity. No ballerina is more graceful. All in all, the whole scene breathes of Springtime — the time of becoming. Both she and the house await completion.

A Woman in Waiting

As an acorn contains the tree,
And seeds have their secrets to share,
A child contains the adult to be —
Only God knows the treasures he planted there.

One young lady, without the clothes,
Without the cheering crowds and excited noise,
Standing still in ballerina pose,
Has put aside many of her childhood toys.

As she enters onto the stage of life,
And awaits the opening of time's door —
Will she be a queen as some man's wife?
Perhaps this and perhaps something more.

What awaits her we hope is good,
In her journey to and through womanhood.

A Bride About to Be

This portrait of a woman about to marry is a study of the primary colors of red, yellow, and blue, and the secondary color of green, and how they enhance her glowing charms of youth and beauty. Although she is seated, she emerges gracefully from her dark background. All of the colors used — from the vase with yellow and red flowers, the fan of blue with flecks of red and white, her earrings, and tiara-like headband — make this an interesting study.

Going beyond the study of colors to a study of her eyes that are so direct and focused, and her lips that are so firm but not frozen, we find a face radiating grace. Really what we find is womanhood in an early stage of development.

Everything considered, the painting is worthy of the woman, the painter, and our study and enjoyment.

The Blossoming Bud

As buds blossoming on a magnolia tree
Exude a beauty that is hard to tell,
A woman who is a bride about to be,
Exudes an unspeakable beauty as well.

Can words, from below or above,
Capture in their non-clay bowls
The wonders of a woman in love?
No, their sides have too many holes.

What words fail to do, a picture might.
It can express so much more than words.
It can open the soul by doors of sight,
And transport us away on the wings of birds.

A woman painted by an artist's skill
Sends within us a resonating thrill.

A Landscape Through an Artist's Eyes

The town Vincent has painted is a typical town in Sicily. With its buildings piled on top of each other, it dominates the hill. Closer to view are people moving on the balcony of a villa or a town's park.

Why is there so much red in the picture? Is it the result of a sunrise or a sunset? No, it is not morning, evening, or any time. It is the artist's time, set by his mood and mind, not a clock.

Actually, the scene is a study where red dominates and blue and violet join forces with it.

What impression does Vincent want you to take away from this painting? Whatever you wish. He would like you to free yourself from your surroundings to place yourself there. Are you detached enough to be able to do that?

The Hill Was Aglow

The sun so bright in the painter's mind,
Turned the hillside into a glowing red.
With a power known only to human kind,
He skillfully puts material time to bed.

His was the time he chose it to be,
And obedient brush did his bidding.
The flourish of colors by his decree
Painted the town like a model sitting.

How mighty are the powers of the artist's brain
That can make a setting live beyond its life.
He can preserve it from wind and rain.
He can create like a husband and wife.

We salute you, artist, so like God,
Who can make special even simple sod.

The Master's View of a Child

The inspiration for this portrait came from a newspaper clipping that caught Vincent's eye. He saw this child, like every child, as a blossom waiting to burst into who and what it would become. Such portraits are in demand because they hold still the child who is quick to change. The old art masters found the child a favorite. They liked to give the child big and striking features. They also liked to circle the child with an ornate frame.

Look at this child closely. Look at the tosseled hair, robust lips, and depth of eyes. See how he or she emerges from the deepest depths of a blue background. Put wings on the child and you would see an angel emerging from the heavens. Oh, the promise and hope this child has for all humanity.

Angels Among Us

A child is an angel without wings,
Recently arrived from an outer blue.
Heavenly trained, he heavenly sings
A song to us unknown and new.

Child from innocence's pool of life,
May those around keep you from harm.
Too quickly and often you are exposed to strife,
With no one to help or sound an alarm.

May it happen one day as the prophet said,
That the lion and lamb, cobra and child
Can sleep and rest in the same bed,
And not make life a jungle wild.

Our eyes are on you, we give you our nod,
That you will be among us as an angel sent by God.

A Mother in Her Wicker Chair

This painting of the 1980's was commissioned by a dentist to be presented to his daughter-in-law. It is a picture of rich, flowing colors that mesmerize the viewer. The woman is beautiful and the child is alert and healthy. It is a delightful picture aimed to catch and please the senses. The greens, blues, and purples of the background make the reds and yellows more exciting. In ways, the picture is on fire.

Obviously the picture is painted in modern ways, but the theme is as old as motherhood. It is a mother savoring her child in ways she could not while the child was within her. Now her quiet, deep emotions of motherhood and adoration of life find expressions in the object of her baby and love.

A Young Mother's Love

The bond between a mother and child,
That begins when a child begins,
Comes from an instinct old and wild
That is programmed so that it always wins.

The bond is intense but not yet deep,
It will take years and deeds to grow.
It is like truths waiting to be rooted in sleep,
That take years and deeds to know.

For now mother and child your bond is secure.
Like being in love, you are sure it will last.
It will take storms and holding on to mature,
To firm it up in a strong steel cast.

Hail to mother's love whether young or old,
One has the shine, the other the value of gold.

Once Again at Her Tasks

This scene of his mother at the sewing machine before the window was one Vincent saw often. Like Rembrandt who often used his mother as a subject of his paintings, Vincent sought to make this domestic scene come alive by contrasting colors, lights, and the vertical and horizontal positioning of the elements within the room.

The colors he uses are many. They give the painting distance and closeness, and they tend to draw us into the setting. The outside and inside light and dark areas give the painting substance. The vertical positions of the window, his mother and her chair, and the horizontal positions of the sewing machine lid top, the shades, and the bed give the painting structure.

All in all, these contrasts turn a simple domestic scene into a warm, cherished one.

What Love Will Do

Many are the promises of what love will do —
The devotion, the gifts, the travels far —
All of these are given to assure love is true.
One might even promise the other a star.

A mother's love is shown all of her days,
Not by toys, jewels, or a costly thing,
But by deeds and so many unseen ways,
That lasso her loved ones into a ring.

A son's love is not shown by swimming a sea,
Or by the big dangerous deeds he dares,
Or by the gifts around the Christmas tree,
But by the tenderness that shows he cares.

Vincent, your art has honored your mother well,
More, much more than words can ever tell.

Mother and Child

Based on what he had seen on a subway of a mother and how an older child controlled the younger child, Vincent transferred this element of control to the country and to a mother over her very active child.

In this outdoor scene the leaves of a tree are spaced to allow the sun to filter through upon a mother and child. There is a glimpse of a town on the left and an arbor of grapes above the two. Notice the richness of the colors used to lowlight and highlight the setting of the scene.

The scene is an American version of an English style of painting children in action.

Free and Restricted

Child, learn a lesson wise —
To be free but held within a firm hold.
Like a kite, reach for the skies,
But be grounded in things better than gold.

What are the securing roots you need?
They start with the clasp of your mother's arms;
They will grow, like you, with every good deed.
These assure your freedom from all harms.

Good mother, the treasure you hold is great.
He is filled with childhood glee.
Teach him to love and not to hate.
Hold him firm but carefully free.

Child and mother, tremendous as a team,
Enjoy each other with love's fondest gleam.

The Blue Enfanta

As a great admirer of great schools of art, Vincent takes his inspiration for this painting of his grandniece from the Spanish Court painters. Being "court" painters, they have their subjects dressed in robes of royalty, and although they might be very young, they are given grownup qualities.

This painting is obviously a Christmas scene. Wrapped gifts abound under the decorated tree. The child, with young unsure eyes, is holding a Christmas ornament in her hand. It is as if one day she would hold a good part of the world in her hands. The colors of the painting are rich and regal.

Unless You Become

The Rabbi Jesus said long ago,
When speaking of pride and its guile,
You cannot put your foot, or even your toe,
Into the kingdom, unless you become a child.

What Jesus is asking is to retain within
The simple style of childhood ways,
And not to replace innocence with sin,
But to live humbly all our days.

As the Spanish conquerors sought gold
To enrich the kingdom's wealth,
The art masters painted children as old,
With thoughts of presenting an ideal health.

If from the two, one I had to choose,
The overgrown child I would seek to lose.

Eyes That Say So Much

This portrait of a tennis player is based on a picture Vincent saw in a newspaper. The woman's eyes caught his eyes, and he knew he had to paint her. He did not have to follow where her eyes were looking, but he knew he had to look deeply into the spirit hovering her Mona Lisa type look. The smile in her eyes and on her cheeks gave her a solemnity that intrigued him and inspired him to use his artistic talents to show his vision of her to others. He has succeeded to do this by his use of both cold and warm red colors. His use of values of blue add their special touch. Gaze at her and catch her spirit and Vincent's vision of her.

A Woman's Look

Like lamps our eyes give us a look,
That is more than vision and sight.
They can be open covers of a book
That bathe one's face with inner light.

Look at the eyes of this lady fair.
Where are they looking, what do they see?
Is there or is there not someone there
Who steadies her eyes with glee?

Woman firm is your beauty and grace.
They reflect the reality of a noble mind.
They speed like light into outer space,
And yet they leave their treasures behind.

Because my soul you have softened,
I will return to drink of you often.

Portrait of a Wife

A husband, very much in love with his young bride, wanted to perpetuate her beauty in the style of John Singer Sargeant, one of America's great portrait painters.

Everyone was pleased with the results of this life-size portrait.

The scene is rich and luscious. It flows with grandeur. It glows. Sitting on a large sofa that abounds with pillows and a cocktail table on the left, the woman is resplendent with light and beauty. She is young womanhood personified.

Take note, if you wish to, and look for Vincent's portrait that is cleverly concealed but sufficiently revealed between the two candles in the background.

What Words Cannot Say

When beauty blossoms with fresh blooms,
All the world stands still to stare.
When a woman's beauty fills a room,
Describing words are bony and bare.

Words cannot echo fitting sounds
Of what is beyond their reach.
They shoot high but fall to the ground
Because of the limitations of speech.

But cheerful colors are not such cripples,
They run, they rush, they seek to convey,
Not statically, but in flowing ripples,
That beauty is like a sunny day.

With the catching charms of eyes and lips,
Woman, your grace is more than sailing ships.

Mixing the Old and New

This painting, so like the old Dutch Masters, is a sample of Vincent's ability to mix the old and the new.

Vincent does not slavishly copy those who inspire him. He adds his own personal touches to his work. Like the old Dutch Masters, Vincent uses the balance and uniformity they used in their paintings. Regardless of the setting, the ceilings are high and the floors are decorated with an elaborate pattern. The people are quaint and dressed in stylish ways.

Look at the yellow and orange colors that soften and warm the portrait you are viewing. The stripes of black make the other colors stand out the more. Obviously it is a home that knows culture. Would you like to visit it? Why not do so by entering and relaxing there in your imagination.

Another Time, Another Place

How often in thought have you flown
To times and places of the past —
Not as a child, but one full grown —
To savor experiences you hope will last?

Within us deep a dreamer hides,
Whether we are fast asleep or wide awake,
Who can take us for a dreamer's ride,
An adventure only a dreamer can make.

So travel to Holland of years ago,
Walk comfortably within this portrait's door.
Feel its warmth and gentle glow,
Absorb its charm and so much more.

Enter this home, as if on a loan,
Visit it often as if it were your own.

Color My World Red

Vincent calls this portrait a rhapsody in red.

It is a portrait inspired by the commissioned portrait of the woman Eve which we have entitled UNLIKE THE ORIGINAL EVE.

The painting is a fascinating work of art because of its use of warm and cold reds. The red in the woman is warm. The background is cold. She is stationary. The background is in constant movement. It looks like she will be immersed into her background.

What is most interesting about this portrait is how it captured Vincent's mood. The color is his mood. It goes where it wants. It is on fire, and yet it is not consumed because of the blue and the baseboard. It is Vincent capturing the woman's vitality by letting loose of his own surging, even screaming, vitality.

If you can, try to catch its fire.

On Fire But Not Consumed

When Moses gazed on a bush on fire,
And wondered why it was not burned,
Was it because his sight was a liar,
Or was it that he had so much to learn?

As you gaze on this fire from Vincent's brushes,
And are caught up in its swirling mirth,
Are your eyes blurred by its red rushes,
Or do you come away with a new birth?

Gaze on, gaze on, it will not swallow you up.
Focus on her face and let the mystery grow.
Fill your eyes and mind, as a spilling cup.
Let yourself be captured somewhere in your soul.

In life it is better not to hold too tight,
When dealing with the flowers of fantasy's flight.

In the Service of Her Country

This portrait of Captain Susan Blake, like all of Vincent's paintings, has a story to it.

One day Vincent received an obituary of Susan Blake from her two daughters. With the obituary was a note saying that they had wanted to contact him to ask him to do something special for their mom to surprise her for her 80th birthday. Unfortunately, their mom had gotten sick and died before the contact had been made.

He recognized that the picture of Susan in the obituary was from a half-length portrait he had done for her, and decided to surprise the family with a full-length painting of her. The picture here is a copy of the painting Vincent did and sent to the family. They loved it.

In the painting, notice Susan's eyes and facial expression. Her promotion to captain meant a great deal to Susan, and she shows it. Vincent held Susan in such regard, he wanted her to live on, not only in his memory, but also in his portrait.

Lasting Impressions

Impressions can be surface or deep,
Like shooting comets or fixed stars.
Some are placed in vaults to keep,
Others are placed in disposable jars.

What special treats, special meetings can be.
They are gifts of gems beyond compare.
They are worth traveling land and sea.
They are that special, they are that rare.

The poet, the artist, and also you
Have met special others, I am sure,
Who have impressed you in ways so true,
You know beyond doubt they will endure.

Such warmth, such light, such people give,
That even when dead they continue to live.

The Laughed-At Dwarf

During his more than six decades of painting, Vincent's works have followed the pendulum's swing from objects that are ordinary to those that are not.

In this painting, Vincent's swing of the pendulum is far out and far back. He is presenting a theme that was classical in old Spanish courts. It is that of a dwarf playing a musical instrument. It is one that features sick humor. The more grotesque the dwarf was, the more laughter he provoked.

Vincent steps beyond his ordinary self to use cubes and prisms to present us a basketful of colors. Reds and blues predominate. Look closely and carefully at the dwarf's eyes. He, who is the brunt of other's sick humor, shows his inner sadness through the openings of his eyes.

Not All Humor is Funny

Oh humans, often good, sometimes cruel,
You are capable of the noblest deeds.
But at times there is a duel,
When the bad, the ugly succeeds.

Is it not enough when nature fails
To bring forth a good image of God?
Why do you go full steam or sail
To pounce on one whose form is odd?

Laughed-at dwarf of a royal hall,
Where humor was confused with poking fun,
It is like pushing a person to fall,
Or like chasing a drunk to make him run.

In this life you are filled with grief,
In eternal life you will find relief.

Albert Verdone

This portrait of Albert Verdone in 1983 was a natural for Vincent to paint. He was impressed by this man of aristocratic Spanish and Sicilian stock. Albert grew up in a background of culture.

Albert was a proud, handsome man who wanted to be a concert violinist, but he was not good enough to achieve this goal. Not able to make a career of music, he ended up as a pharmaceutical salesman.

Notice in Vincent's painting how proudly Albert holds his violin, and how Vincent's use of green and supporting colors help you to enter more fully into this powerful painting, and especially into Albert's eyes.

The Art of Aging

Age has a way to paint its lines
On the canvas of our body and face.
Each stroke, so heavenly-humanly defines
The rich beauty of God's grace.

This beauty is not restricted to any age,
But reaps its harvest when we are old.
Then wisdom can make of us a sage —
A treasure more precious than gold.

How deep the eyes of one in the winter of life,
How set and strong his lips and chin!
Each line has been formed by encountered strife,
Not into a bursting smile but a meaningful grin.

Each of us, whether painted green and blue,
Reflects God's beauty, ever ancient, ever new.

A Brother's Pride

Vincent's pride in his sister Dolly, the wife of Fred our photographer, is visible in his portrayal and placement of her in cultured Spanish dress. He is following the lead of the great Spanish Masters.

The Spanish, especially in conquering other lands, often showed a dark side in their lives and paintings. In his portrait of his sister, Vincent casts her into a somber setting to bring out her deep dignity. The blue mantilla on her head and the dark background enhance her distinguished features. She looks royal. Her hair is alive with color and movement, her nose skis gracefully off her face, and her eyes, so distant and near, make her a queen in the creative land/realm of imagination. She is indescribably beautiful, in art and in fact.

Lady in Mantilla Blue

How stately she sits and looks
At admirers she knows not.
More eloquently than words in books,
She mixes passions of cold and hot.

Woman, so filled with wordless words,
How can we give you a name?
Mighty as stampeding herds,
To label you would be to our shame.

Oh lady worthy of mighty raves,
With lips so firm and red,
And hair like strong ocean waves,
You have thrilled many a heart and head.

Many are the delights God has revealed,
Woman, in you, many of them are sealed.

Resting From Her Labors

Off and on Vincent worked on this painting of his mother some 40 years. His heart wanted to say so much, perhaps more than art is capable of expressing. How does a son express his sentiments and gratitude to such a good mother? He tries but never really succeeds.

Vincent captures this image of his ailing mother one afternoon while she lay sleeping with her bath robe of green and blue and her coverlet of red and streaks of blue covering her from her waist down. Vincent found a serene, floating look on her that he wanted to impose on his painting of her. He gave his color-filled imagination such a free rein that his composition rises above ordinary reality. It takes him, and us, to a level of life that has no boundaries. He shows this with his lavish use of yellow, green and red.

A Rest Beyond Sleep

Sleep on dear mother in peaceful slumber.
Sleep on and from your life's work rest —
Not as one cutting through hard wood lumber —
But as one who deserves the very best.

How does a son such labors repay,
When the debt is so enormously high?
He cannot because there is no way
His gratitude can reach to the sky.

The answer unto love is love's return,
Whether we are ordinary or super smart.
Love is more than anyone can earn,
It repays with an exchange of the heart.

Rest on mother, in that where labors cease,
Rest on mother, with merited eternal peace.

The Merry-Go-Round

This large painting was commissioned to portray five children in a different, non-conventional way.

See how the children vary in the presentations of themselves. One day they will leave this merry-go-round, this circle of family life, to go on their own, but for now they are rejoicing in their merriment. Bathe in the warm light of this rich collection of colors.

Obviously this painting, from the horses to the hunched cat, is well-studied and well-presented. It is meant to activate our memory and imagination. Hopefully we were once gleeful like these children. If not then, be so now as you enter into this portrait.

When Laughter Ripples

Oh for the light joys of youth,
How we long to make them last.
We place them in a keyless booth,
To safeguard the joys of our past.

But life moves on at its pace,
We can try but not stop its flow.
Each moment is laden with its grace,
As to endless eternity we go.

Does carefree laughter cease and stop
As we make our way to our goal?
It can as we labor to reach the top,
But let it not, it is good for our soul.

So children store memories light,
To sustain you in the winter of night.

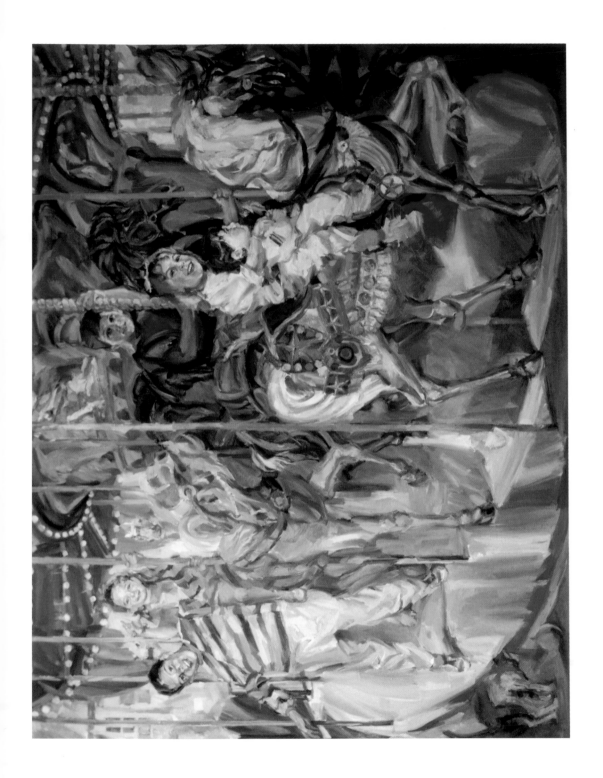

An Artist's Dream in Paint

At a glance this picture of a young bride who is sitting back and fixing her hair and hat is like a hazy mirror reflection. It needs a close look to see her hands and seated position. Her face is catchy and clear.

But to look for the pieces of the portrait is to miss the beauty of the composition. The beauty is in the flow of the predominately yellow color and its complementary greens, blues, reds, oranges, etc. They are a razzle-dazzle flow of movement. Although it appears to be a casual picture, it is not. It is well designed and arranged. Enjoy.

To Be Feminine

To be feminine is to have a flow,
That floods a woman's body and being.
It is almost impossible for a man to know.
It is there, visible but barely seen.

Oh how the wells of life seep within,
And give you the bearing of a royal grace.
The life that flows so near your skin
Contributes so much to the human race.

Well have artists chosen you to paint,
Your colors are many and bright.
Whether dancing or at prayer as a saint,
Your being radiates with light.

Woman, God has gifted us when he gave you life,
Whether you are single or a happy man's wife!

A Questioning Little Girl

Staring at you is an uncertain, sad, even pouting 2 1/2 year old little girl whose mood is partially reflected in her doll that lies limp on the floor.

The whole composition of this portrait is a marvelous study of green and blue colors. With the help of the light coming from outside, these colors bounce off each other and give a sense of movement. There is action and inter-reaction in the portrait.

The child is a study in herself. Her finger on her chin and the shadows across her face and eyes leave us puzzled. She seems to be caught between disappointment and unhappiness. She is tasting, and perhaps testing, an unpleasant moment of life. Who said childhood is always carefree and sunny?

Life Starts Early

Where do the curved marks of questions set in?
When do we stop not knowing what to do?
It starts, not knowing how to win,
When we are young, even only two.

This scene is adulthood in miniature —
A little girl in blue blond curls,
All dressed up and all unsure,
Is caught up in colorful whirls.

Why is she sad and in a pouting mood?
Has she been deprived of a strong desire?
Why does she feel she has to brood?
Where is her smile and cheerful fire?

All of these questions we can stack high,
None of them will stop her need to cry.

Unlike the Original Eve

This commissioned portrait by Vincent is about Eve, one who has survived great trials. To survive these ordeals required all of Eve's spirit and fortitude. Both would serve her well in caring for her sick husband who unfortunately did not have the opportunity to see the completed portrait of the woman he loved and adored.

This portrait is stunningly beautiful because of Eve and the background she chose for it. Her reflected profile in the mirror shows a side view of her stately face. She flows with grace.

Wearing her favorite dress and choosing the background, Eve oozes with vitality. Adding the wrought iron bench enhances the painting's splendor by mixing in a certain amount of casualness to it all.

Eve, unlike the first Eve, you are a credit to womanhood and to the whole human race.

A Courageous Woman

A courageous heart has a beauty of its own,
Especially when growing among thorny weeds.
Despite the disadvantages of where it is sown,
It produces unnoticed notable deeds.

Hail Eve, looking from your portrait view,
Who knows what hurts hide behind your eyes?
Hatreds few could ever guess humanity knew
Have scorched your throat with soundless cries.

You look so regal on your iron throne,
Where you command with your half stare.
You have a royalty that not many have known.
I fear that much of you is elsewhere.

Whether focusing on the future or past,
May courage be with you to the very last.

When Life Seemed More Picturesque

Once again, using the style and skills of the old Dutch Master, Vincent shifts his attention from a purely domestic scene to a more commercial one. It is the scene of a shop where one patron, standing, is being served. Another patron, sitting, is waiting to be served.

The scene is interesting because of the people in it. On the left is a little girl who is unsure of herself. On the right is a woman with a basket who is pausing to look at the little girl to give her a clue of what to do.

The scene is also interesting because its light is coming from the window. Look how warmly it brightens the room. Look how skillfully it works on the floor pattern.

To enter the scene fully is like taking off to another delightful time and place. The journey is reasonable and the rewards are great.

Lasting Wealth

Most look on the riches of energy and health
As the pearls to be cherished in every way.
They, more than gold, are treasured as wealth.
The ongoing search is how to make them stay.

Wealth is real wealth when it endures
And weathers the erosions of biting time.
It takes the mind on magical tours
And lifts it beyond to what is sublime.

When reality is enhanced by an artist's skills,
It becomes more than a magical wand.
It becomes the glowing gold of ripe wheat fields.
It becomes the stage of a fresh, eternal dawn.

So, Vincent, we hail you for filling us with glee,
And helping us to see what only an artist can see.

Moses, Radiant With God

This painting of Moses was done for a Jewish doctor. It is a study of light.

According to the Scripture, Moses was so filled with light after his encounter with God, he had to wear a veil over his face (Exodus 34, 29-35). Vincent has taken away that veil and has made this painting as bright as a rainbow, the filtered colors found in white light. The secondary color of green predominates in the painting.

This is a gentle, non-judgemental Moses who Vincent has emerged from the Jewish Star of David which actually did not exist at the time of Moses. One of his eyes is red, the other is green They have a puzzled look to them. He is wondering about the people's ability and willingness to keep the commandments written in Hebrew and which he is holding so dearly. As we know, they often did not keep them.

In the Presence of God

Oh, Moses, most privileged of men,
How great and radiant is your being!
You truly rank as a number ten,
Especially after the Mount Sinai scene.

What was it like meeting face to face
With the almighty who cannot be seen?
Was it the exuberance of his grace
That splashed you with colors, especially green?

You truly are a man of all ages,
Because you are ageless with enduring light.
You are the mountain top of sages.
How mystical must have been your sight.

Help us to learn your rules of life,
To escape outer and inner strife.

A Christmas Card

Vincent describes this scene painted in 1974 as a commercial design. Its intended use was as a Christmas card. It is that and more. It is a classical presentation of a most holy scene and fact. The fact is the humanization of God in the form of Jesus, the Christ.

Obviously, while being the same as most Christmas cards and their presentation of the birth of Jesus, it is different. It is typical of the late Renaissance painters. Notice the framed throne and the framed foreground of the painting. It is like a church setting. All of this is boxed in by another ornate frame. Also notice the brilliance of the colors that clothe the two.

In many ways the painting is like an icon, a painting that invites you to enter with devotion and love.

The Setting Matters Not

Whether pictured in a noisy scene
Of mooing animals and piles of hay,
Or in a place so much more serene,
We reverence this most holy day.

It is the day the Lord has made,
He made it before he made time.
It is the scene of a humble maid
Submitting to a calling so sublime.

Oh child so scared and holding tight
To the woman who gave you birth,
What do you see beyond your sight —
Is heaven so different from earth?

To you, brave mother, and to your son,
Thanks for a mission so nobly done.

Looking Through Special Eyes

In painting this Christmas scene, Vincent is influenced by the old Renaissance masters. It is a scene filled with artistic touches.

Not only does the scene contrast the majesty of God with a lowly stable, it contrasts the rich and the poor, the old and the young, humans and animals. They all gather around this child as if they are gathering around a bonfire.

Further artistic touches are the cool red colors, the green of Joseph's robes, the orange of the cows, and the white of the infant's clothes. Some of the light comes from the lantern, but most of it comes from the infant and his mother. The colors and light give the scene an almost unreal look.

This portrait is a credit to Vincent and the old masters who have inspired him.

Many Are the Attempts

When something as big and utterly real,
As happened one night in an animal stable,
Many will try to place their seal
And render it as best as they are able.

Oh blessed light, not from a star,
From God who generates all being,
We have some sight of who you are,
But most remains hidden and unseen.

Oh bless the artists and their skills,
Who stroke after stroke with their hand —
Like grinding, grinding grain mills —
Produce what is helpful and exquisitely grand.

Thank you for lifting us like a dove
To what is beyond and far above.

Flight Into Egypt

Looking at this biblical scene of the flight into Egypt by the holy family of Joseph, Mary, and Jesus, one is invited to enter into it. It is like looking at a tapestry.

The spirals that give the background depth and the abundance of the refreshing color of green make the painting a kind of mystical celebration of the poverty and flight of the couple and child.

In a marvelous but humble way, Vincent portrays a much revered doctrine of the faith of Mary as a queen who is holding her son, the Prince of the world. Both mother and son have halos. Joseph the protector does not, and yet he is dressed in fine fashion to show his dignity in the trio of the holy family.

With Hurried Steps

At times in life we must speed our steps,
When danger draws near like a hound.
With hearts heavy and with regrets,
We need an escape to be safe and sound.

A family of old was made alert
To threats to their child's life.
With his heart overweighted with heavy hurt,
A man fled his country with child and wife.

Why do humans have to be that way,
Will anger and violence never cease?
Can hatred not be held at bay,
So we can live with one another in peace?

In this life dangers will always be,
And with hurried steps often we will have to flee.

Art and Agony

In an art contest, in the Army in 1944 when he was a soldier, Vincent sketched this aerial view of the crucifixion of Christ long before Salvador Dali painted his.

In this painting, done years later from his sketch, Vincent tries to capture the deep agony of Christ and the women onlookers. They are contrasted with matter-of-fact ways of those who carry out their assigned task. The scene is strong but not over-sentimental.

From the vertical positions of the people, the cross, and the ladder, and the richness of the red and other colors that convey the feelings of torture and pain, the scene is one of conceived design. It is trying to show man's inhumanity to man on the best representatives of humans, Jesus the Rabbi of Nazareth.

Were You There?

Of old a song asks of our presence
When they crucified the man of Galilee.
Unhesitantly we plead our absence
At this inhuman assault on humanity.

Although hammerless did we hit the nails
That wed him as a spouse to the wood?
Did we join with the "crucify him" hails
That put to death one so good?

Look at the torture, listen to the cries,
See the blood spilling in spurts of red.
Let your caring reach the skies
In appreciation for the blood he shed.

If not then, let us now be there,
To comfort God as he hangs in mid air.

Although there can be no final words about the uplifting importance art can have on our lives, we will close this book with a comment about art and reality.

The artist, like the poet and others, encounters the realities everyone experiences, but he does it differently. Looking through the eyes of his imagination, feelings, and mind — not only his physical eyes — he sees more. He often sees past the hard surfaces of reality to a softness that is concealed. If the softness is not there, he can put it there by his use of colors and light. He does not run away from what is. He simply suggests what could be.

In the paintings in this book Vincent's intention is to lift us, at least for a time, to feast on colors and light that enrich the soul. Hopefully his efforts and the book have helped to accomplish that.